SACRED EARTHWALK:
WISDOM OF THE ELDERS

The Secret for transforming life's conflicts, hardships, and struggles to a life filled with honesty, humility, courage, respect, generosity, wisdom, and unconditional love.

Jerzy Kokurewicz

Jerzy M. Kokurewicz

ISBN: 978-0-9986327-1-1 (Paperback)

First Edition –June 2020

Website: https://www.jerzymkokurewicz.com

ACKNOWLEDGMENTS

This book is dedicated to Heather who gave me reason to realize my visions and dreams. And to my sister, Annette, who is and continues to be the bedrock of our family.

And to the Elders who guided my journey:
Lillian Pitawanakwat, Whitefish River First Nation;
William Commanda, Kitigan Zibi First Nation;
Leona Jacobs, Garden River First Nation

Heartfelt thanks for making this book a reality:
David Bruce Leonard, Dr. Stefan J. Malecek, Lawrence Taylor, and Anne Guchuhi.

Jerzy M. Kokurewicz

DISCLAIMER

T he author of this book does not prescribe the use of any technique as a form of treatment for physical, emotional or medical problems without the advice of a physician either directly or indirectly. The author is only sharing information of a general nature to help you in your quest for your emotional, physical or spiritual wellbeing.

TABLE OF CONTENTS

Acknowledgements iii

Disclaimer v

Forward x

Author's Note xii

Prophecy of the Seventh Fire 1

Preface 3

Introduction 7

1st Grandfather Teaching- Honesty 11

2nd Grandfather Teaching-Humility 21

3rd Grandfather Teaching-Courage 31

4th Grandfather Teaching-Respect 43

5th Grandfather Teaching-Generosity 51

6th Grandfather Teaching-Wisdom 63

7th Grandfather Teaching-Love 71

Choices *81*

Embodiment *83*

Begin with Honesty *85*

Embrace Humility *89*

Have Courage *91*

Respect All That Is *95*

Be Infinitely Generous *99*

Grow Wise *103*

Love Unconditionally *105*

Ode'imin Teaching *111*

Epilogue *115*

About the Author *116*

References *117*

Unconditional Love is not only what we must practice.

It is also what we must always try to receive.

Sacred EarthWalk: Wisdom of the Elders

FORWARD

In our "post-truth" era, we are told that there are no greater truths, that everything is relative. We are told that any map we choose to follow is as good as any other. So, we drift without a compass, chasing knowledge and information as if it were a life raft. But, our lives remain empty, and we are still adrift. Knowledge is not wisdom.

But, for hundreds of thousands of years, our ancestors had a map, an inner and outer compass that they received from their ancestors, the Elders of their tribe. They, in turn received it from their Elders, and so on. Luckily, this map has not been lost.

Jerzy Kokurewicz spent many years sitting at the feet of the Keepers of Wisdom, honoring them and the maps they entrusted him with. The truths he has been honored to share are not relative, nor are they disposable. They are the distillation of hundreds of thousands of years of pain, suffering, redemption, joy, and love. They contain the truth of what it means to be a human being.

It is said that in the kingdom of the blind, the one-eyed are kings. Our Elders' most fervent wish is for us to open our eyes, both of them, and see.

David Bruce Leonard, L.Ac.
Founder of the Earth Medicine Institute
Author of <u>Medicine at Your Feet: Healing Plants of the Hawaiian Kingdom</u>

AUTHOR'S NOTE

I did not get here on my own. This is not a vision that resides exclusively within me and my being. A true storyteller can only tell you about things that somehow all of us already know. Otherwise, how could these weavers of imagination touch you so deeply?

My Elder, Lillian Pitawanaqwat of the Whitefish River First Nation, Birch Island, Ontario, loved me. She was the one that told me of these Teachings. And, in so doing so, she always encouraged me and guided me to find my own vision, my own path, my own story. Did anything written here about the Teachings come from her? No. She simply gave me the framework. My dreams and visions filled it.

My Elder, William Commanda of the Kitigan Zibi Anishinabeg First Nation was a true Mishomis (Grandfather) to me. He let me into his life quietly, loved me greatly with just a few words, and called me his best friend. This humble, intelligent man was a true Human Being. He shared with me his shortcomings, as well as his brilliance,

My third Elder, Leona Jacobs of Garden River First Nations, was joy and love in human form. There is never any doubt as *to the unconditional nature of her love. It shone through her eyes and her smile even as the pains of her body humbled her. She too loved me, and I her.*

The communities of Whitefish River First Nation, and Kitigan Zibi First Nation have never failed to show me respect and love, regardless of my skin color. The unfailing generosity I experience when I visit my adopted family is like a wonderful warm summer rain, refreshing and nourishing.

Jerzy M. Kokurewicz

PROPHECY OF THE SEVENTH FIRE

"In the time of the Seventh Fire, New People will emerge. They will retrace their steps to find what was left by the trail. Their steps will take them to the Elders who they will ask to guide them on their journey. ... The task of the New People will not be easy."

"If the New People will remain strong in their quest, the Water Drum of the Midewiwin Lodge will again sound its voice. There will be a rebirth of the Anishinabe Nation and a rekindling of old flames. The Sacred Fire will again be lit."

from The Mishomis Book - The Voice of the Ojibway, by Eddie Benton-Banai.[1]

Jerzy M. Kokurewicz

PREFACE

___

There are many paths to Understanding, which implies connection and unity. To seek Enlightenment is to set yourself apart, have something others do not have. Whereas to seek Understanding is to invite a meeting, and a confluence of inner worlds, both Human and non-Human, seen and unseen.

The Aboriginal Peoples of Turtle Island offer one such path of Understanding known as the Medicine Wheel.

There are many Medicine Wheel Teachings shared in the Lodge or in Ceremony. One of these is known as the Grandfather Teachings. These Teachings contain the wisdom that the Elders of a community are expected to pass along to the Seven Generations that are to follow.

Honesty, Humility, Courage, Respect, Generosity, Wisdom, and Love are the Seven Teachings of the Grandfather. These Seven Teachings are a guide for the young, as well as a reminder for the mature of what are the most important attributes of living a beneficial and wholesome life. Additionally, these Seven Teachings form the foundational knowledge for effective and wise Eldership, as well as a *template for developing strong foundations of leadership.*

For tens of thousands of years, these and other Medicine Wheel Teachings were imparted through the oral traditions of the Anishinabeg People (the original inhabitants of the Eastern woodlands and the far North of Turtle Island). They were transmitted orally in recognition that all Teachings are sacred and alive, and to honor their vitality and relevance. Thus, each Elder imparted a bit of their own spirit and unique insight into these Teachings every time these Teachings were expressed. The Teachings grew and matured as they were conveyed to their peers and the generations to come.

The dominant culture in which we are currently embroiled has few quiet gathering places. The stories we are subjected to are more sensational than wise. There are no fires to sit by and spend a pleasant evening quietly chatting with our loved ones. It is becoming exceedingly rare to find a small grandchild sitting in our lap, eager to know what we know, full of questions that fuel not only their own growth and maturity, but ours as well.

Now we use written words to transmit knowledge and ideas. But it is of paramount importance that we acknowledge the dangers and limitations of the written word. Words that appear on paper or parchment have always had a special, peculiar power.   It is the power of implied commitment and eternal constancy. Perhaps that is one of the roots of our outrage when a treaty is broken, or a signed agreement is abrogated. We hold the written word as a power not to be trifled with, even though we never stop trifling with it.

As you read these words, my advice to you is this: Treat the words of this written message as a breath frozen in time. Breathe these words in and be sure to let them melt into your being. Make them your own. Give them the power of Life by allowing them to grow within you in a wise and loving way. Never spit these words out exactly as you received them. That would be unwise and disrespectful to the spirits that are lovingly calling you to clarity, understanding, and ultimately joy.

What you are reading now are simply my words made into the visual symbols that fuel the inner voice we all hear. The words written here are not the truth. And they are not lies. They are simply a finger pointing to the Moon.

INTRODUCTION

Picture this.

Thousands of generations ago you might have been sitting by a fire while your mother was preparing a meal. Your father was away, hunting with the other men of your tribe. But your grandfather was with you by the fire, sitting, busy mending a tool or something. He looks a lot like your father, but is quieter, self-contained. Your grandmother is helping your mother, taking care of your younger siblings, chatting away with the other grandmothers that came to visit.

This is your family and tribe. All of these people have been with you since the day you were born. They have been with you every day of your life, every hour of your life. There are no mysteries between you and your family. Without any conscious effort the qualities of their individual natures are thoroughly known and embodied in your being.

Regard your grandfather for a moment. He has had many experiences that you have not had yet, but you know that those experiences and more are in your future. He knows how to get along by himself in the wilderness and how to get *along with the other members of his community. He has proved all he needs to prove. He is respected for his wisdom and cherished for his stories. He has walked the path of a human being and done it well.*

In the time that we now occupy you no longer have the privilege of sitting by a fire night after night with your cherished grandfather. As it is for most of us, your time with your grandfather is fleeting, maybe a couple of times a year, during holidays at best. There is no quiet absorption of his wisdom and spirit, if indeed there is any that you can easily discern. There's an initial "Hello!", some chatter, hopefully some comfort, and too soon "Goodbye, Grandpa! See you next year!" And even this scenario is relatively rare.

However, some wisdom, even if it is difficult to perceive, is helpful in as much as there is always the potential for deeper roots to develop. Many of us had to learn to respect the fire through the burning of our own flesh, either figuratively or literally. But even the quietest and most distant Grandfather desires to pull us away from the flame as if to say, "Learn from me, my child."

If I was your Grandfather and you sincerely wanted to live a better way of life, then this is what I would tell you. Follow these Teachings. Embody these Teachings, even though you don't know where they will take you. Let these Teachings imbue you with the smoke and comfort of that fire from tens of thousands of years ago.

It's true that much has changed in the last hundred thousand generations. And yet there are some very important things that have remained. We are still breathing the same Air that kept our ancestors alive. We are still sustaining ourselves with the bounty of the same Earth, cleansing ourselves with the same Waters, and spending our days under the very same Sun that our forebears enjoyed.

And, perhaps most importantly, our inner yearning to be a better Human Being, a more purposeful Human Being, and a happier Human Being has never changed.

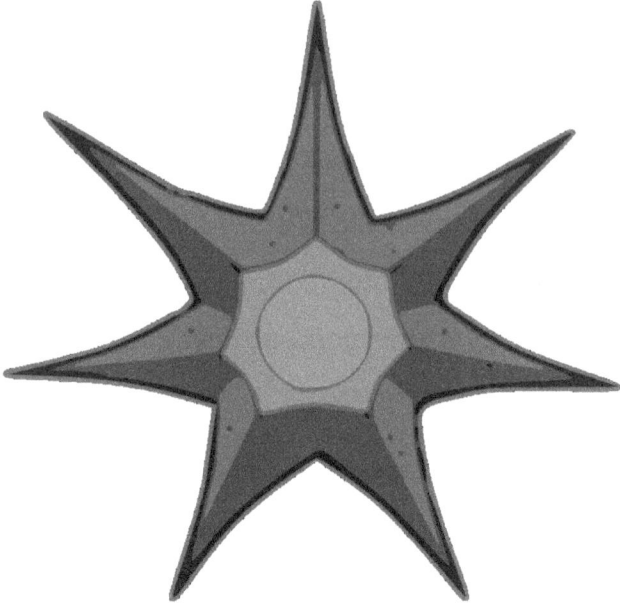

THE FIRST GRANDFATHER TEACHING

HONESTY

We have all heard this:

*L*ife is a journey, not a destination. Journeys are wonderful things, with all the discoveries of our meandering. And while journeys may or may not have a destination, all journeys have direction. How important is it to sense and perhaps cultivate that direction?

Imagine this.

You are alone, soaked to the bone, lost in a dark raging storm. You need to get to safety, but all you have is a wind-whipped map in your hand. Your map shows you where home is, but where exactly are you on the map? You look again through the blinding rain trying to figure out where you are and trying to guess in what direction you can find shelter. But what if you are wrong? What if where you think you are on the map is wrong? In that case your map will never help you get to where you need to be. Any direction you pick will be wrong with possible disastrous results.

A physical map is simply a general interpretation of the world that you are surrounded by and what you hope lies *beyond the next rise. In envisioning your life as a map, the events of the past (which are the landmarks of your existence) appear real enough, but too often your perception of them is often obscured by the mist of pain and misunderstanding. All of us need to learn that pain and the misunderstandings created by that pain are only passing storms we are in the midst of trying to survive and are unreliable starting points for our journey to safety and wholeness.*

Truth-telling is an important discipline, but that is not all of what Honesty is about. We all know that someone who tells the truth is not necessarily an honest person. Politicians, advertising executives and lawyers provide us with ample proof of that.

To discover the depth of what Honesty is, we need to learn and experience Creation with our eyes and ears, and through our smell and touch. Our bodies and senses never lie. It is only the stories that we make up in our minds about our sensations that lead us astray.

A map can have much information, but in the end, it is only a rough representation of what is. It is not reality. What we see, hear, touch, and smell is reality, and must not to be confused with our interpretation of what is. Of course there are other facets of real experience that are not discernible with our physical senses, but until we become adept at honestly understanding the physical world around us, how could we ever hope to experience the unseen world without distortion?

A good map will always show us landmarks; easily understood markers that help us see how we got to where we are. On the map of our lives those landmarks are our values, the most vital components of our inner world. The more of these landmarks we can recognize, the more useful our map becomes. We need to know what our values are and, most importantly, to trust our knowing. We need to identify them because they are our inner spirit's food and shelter. We need to learn to recognize them. Experience them. Without embracing our values, we can never reach our destination in the good way that we innately desire.

The map of your life is a very good map in spite of its creases and tears. By embodying the Medicine of Honesty and identifying your values, you can trust that you know where you really are in your life. That deeper Honesty draws you to your values. And deeply realized Honesty is the Medicine that will teach you how to recognize what truly feeds and nourishes your essence.

Now the question is, where are you going? Is your chosen destination compatible with your values? Will you find true safety when you get to your destination, or will you have to endure one hard scramble after another, with no end in sight? Is your destination even on the map of your life?

Ask yourself, are you dictating your destination to Life, perhaps wandering off the path that your values have laid before you? Or can you allow the living world around you to whisper to you what it needs from you?

Allow the noisy storm of your life and pain to settle, so that you can hear the whispers. In that way, you become a partner with Creation. You cease trying to push Life to where it suits you and your unfortunately tainted agenda. You cease putting yourself outside the flowing current of the river of Creation, and avoid getting stuck in the whirlpools and eddies that hold you back.

To think that you can live apart from Life and that you have the strength to divert the stream of Life by your will alone is a lie. And one who lives a lie can never be honest. Perhaps the direction of your life might seem uncomfortable and far too humble, but are you here to satisfy your tainted needs, or to serve Life?

The mission you craft for yourself at the height of the storm might well take you in the wrong direction. But you can only know that when the storm inevitably passes, and the whispers of Life have a chance to be heard. Our destination is our mission. Craft it carefully.

This is deeper Honesty. Without understanding this, nothing else can make sense. Without knowing this, separating fact from fantasy would be impossible.

As our experience of the Medicine of Honesty grows deeper, we become more than mere truth-tellers. We begin to see the whole of Creation as it really is. With our values to guide us, we can clearly see our way home.

A Teaching of the East

The East is where the day begins.

The Eagle welcomes the Light because he flies the highest and is first to see the rising Sun. The eyes of the Eagle are clear and far-seeing, but he cannot see what there isn't. He can only see what is. He sees the world from horizon to horizon. He can see where you have been, where you are now, and the path you are venturing on. Hiding in the confusion of the underbrush only makes it harder for him to find you and to help you.

There is no wiggle room when it comes to Honesty.

My grandmother's husband, Johnny, was a big, hearty Polish American who played a critical role in bringing my family safe and intact to the United States. He had served as a merchant seaman during the Second World War, with the difficult and dangerous mission of keeping supplies flowing to the Allied armies in Europe. And even though my parents dismissed him as a lowly working class American, he was exceedingly kind and forthright with me, and I idolized him. In my young eyes, there was nothing that could overwhelm this strong giant.

When I was about ten years old I remember he gave me his Merchant Seaman's Handbook, and taught me many useful skills including tying practical and complicated knots and how to coil rope properly so that it could be ready and knot-free at a moment's notice. More than fifty years later, I still utilize the skills he passed onto me.

The most important lesson he taught me was this: Never make excuses. As young as I was, I somehow understood this very clearly.

To accept total responsibility without becoming a victim is a skill that requires absolute honesty. It became a point of pride, and power for me. To even imagine that I, an immigrant youngster, could stand up and say, "Yes, I take full responsibility, and no, I will offer no excuse." was intoxicating.

Honesty, in its fullest, builds strength when it is wielded wisely.

That discipline of not making excuses followed me. I might not have admitted it openly, but no matter what came out of my mouth, my heart always knew where my responsibility lay, even if I did my damndest to avoid it.

Much later, when I traveled the path of recovery from alcohol and emotional addiction, I was confronted with the Tenth Step which states, "(we) continued to take personal inventory and when we were wrong promptly admitted it."

To be the valued and forthright Human Being I imagined I was and could be, there could be no wiggle room.

No excuses.

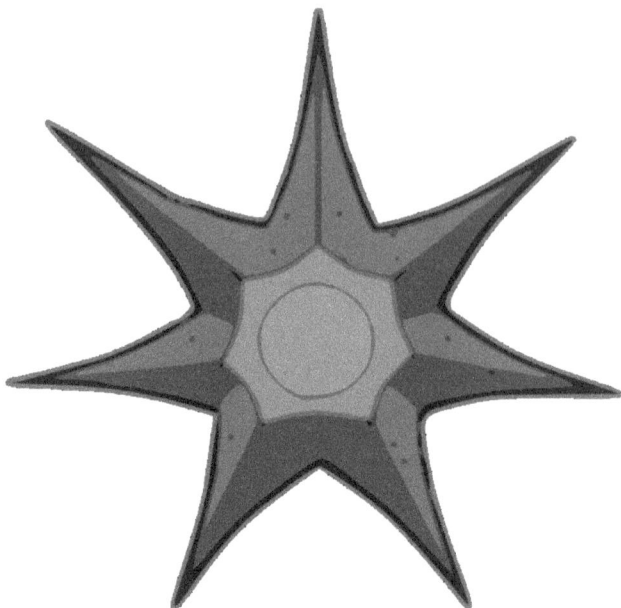

THE SECOND GRANDFATHER TEACHING

HUMILITY

---

*I*n this sorry world ruled by sound bites and ethically challenged over-achievers, humility, as a word and a concept, implies passivity. There is an implication that humility means being boxed in either by our personality or our morals. Any action that is perceived to be outside that imaginary box is summarily and vociferously criticized by all those ethically challenged nitwits who think they are the great arbiters of our dominant culture. The true nature and practice of Humility is enormously threatening to those pitiful bullies' severely wounded inner Spirits.

When you have a clear and honest notion of who you are and begin to see beyond your small world of experiences and sensations, Humility automatically arises. It is often uncomfortable because in this dominant culture, Humility is often confused with vulnerability and denial, the antithesis to a materially rewarding, thus satisfying life. Naturally, none of us want to suffer deprivation. Unfortunately, the message of our current culture is that Humility requires deprivation. Thus, Humility in our culture is not valued.

It is true that Humility does indeed inform us that we are not as great as we might imagine which can be painful to hear.

But there is more.

A deep understanding of Humility also teaches that you are not above nor below any other creation in the Universe. You are no greater than a blade of grass, or a maggot in the compost pile. And at the same time, you are no less than a towering redwood tree or the vast ocean.

Everything has its place. Everything is essential, including you! Nothing is superfluous. Fully and honestly knowing who you are puts you in your rightful and most powerful place as an equal among all the other creations in this infinite Universe. And paradoxically, embodying that power makes room in your life for all the other powerful beings of Creation. That is when you realize your full peership with all the flies and maggots of the world as well as the giants of the Forest.

When you lack Humility there is room for no one in your life but yourself, and by default you become at once the most highly exalted and the most deeply despised occupant in your little universe of one.

The Medicine of Humility expands your life, and never

constricts it. Humility is also an action, but it needs to be held lightly. Adorning yourself with Humility never fails to result in pain and confusion.

That is why truly humble people are very quiet about their Humility. They know that broadcasting their humility will always backfire and will inevitably result in unintended consequences.

It is only in the quiet and humble places of our being that the whispers of Life can be heard. It is in these quiet places that we begin to realize that we are not in charge, and there is a Power greater than ourselves that is responsible for keeping things moving along. All we are responsible for is to play our part and just relax; or at least get out of the way of Life completing itself.

This is how Humility is our shield. The big stuff is never up to us. **We are simply the janitors of Life, sweeping up the rubble of the past to clear the path to the future.**

Confrontation and violence go hand-in-hand. We are told that is how things get done. It is true that things can get accomplished in that way, but how can a reasonable, honest person approve of the heart-breaking harm that has been done to our air, our water, our elders and our children with this violence? One confrontation leads to another, even if it is *in the guise of generosity, and progress. Actions that are not rooted in Humility become confrontations, and confrontations get us nowhere.*

Humility is the antidote to confrontation. Humility is our shield against the corrosion of violence.

Shielded by Humility, we show up, do what we are called to do in the moment, clean things up, and then become quiet again, listening for the whispers of Life.

Of course, our humble actions, quiet as they might be, tend to shout out that we are not slaves to the materialistic paradigm that is destroying our people. Ironically taking on the invisibility of Humility can make us even more visible to those who are tired of drinking the brackish water that this culture offers us, who desire clean, fresh, spiritually refreshing water.

Humility is a place of power. With Humility, we are able to be powerful within our own essence without encroaching on other people's power and not allowing other powers to encroach upon ours.

With Humility, we can remain intact and whole, true to ourselves and the values of our lives. We allow others to have the experiences they need without the interference of our own wounds being projected on them. We can face each other, wounds and all, with equanimity and true compassion.

A Teaching of the South

The South is one end of the great axis around which our Earth spins, *quietly and steadfastly keeping order in our movement towards the new day. There, the spirit of the Turtle waits for us in the ponds of the verdant jungle and the depths of the vast ocean. The shell that keeps her humble also protects her at the same time. When we allow her spirit to walk with ours, her shell deflects those energies that can do us harm, only allowing the light of healing and love into our being. We are assured that within the protection of her shell, we will experience only those things that are necessary for our growth and healing. As uncomfortable as some of those experiences might be for us, we are assured that they will be transformed for our highest good.*

Her shell is her home, and even if she travels far, her sanctuary is always with her.

Our existence is completely out of our control.

My parents were war survivors and refugees. They had to flee their homes in the face of catastrophic events that were out of their control, a story that is still so unfortunately common today.

Most of my mother's family was killed by both the Nazis and the Soviets, leaving her virtually orphaned in the midst of the most horrific catastrophe a young girl could ever experience.

My father and his mother were constantly on the run, fleeing for their lives through Ukraine, Romania, and Austria. They were arrested by the Gestapo at least three times and three times managed to evade death or worse. As a young teenager, homeless and hunted, he stole bags of flour from the hands of the dead to keep him and his mother alive.

I was born in London not long after that war's end. These young people, freshly traumatized and rootless, were my parents. They did their best to create a life for their young family, but the shadow of their war experiences was always there. As a result, I felt a lot of anger and despair about what happened to my family throughout my life. The trauma of war impacted me deeply.

Nearly 50 years after her survival was finally assured with the end of the war, my Mother and I returned to Poland, a trip that she was originally reluctant to take. For three weeks we drove all over the country, visiting where her family had lived, and where she took refuge after participating in the Warsaw Uprising as a young courier for the Armia Krajowa, the Polish underground army, carrying bombs and confidential documents across enemy lines in her book-bag.

When my mother and I visited the memorial museum in Warsaw that documented that hellish ordeal, I was overcome with fierce anger at all those who were responsible for the unimaginable horror that my mother had to endure as such a young girl. I had never felt such deep hatred before in my life, imagining how it must have been to witness the horrifying and unstoppable invasion of armed men who were dedicated to the complete destruction of one's home and culture. The vision of this made me insane.

As I stood on the streets of Warsaw, outside the Museum, tears streaming down my face, I wished with all my heart and soul that Adolf Hitler had never existed so that my mother and the land of my ancestors could be spared this unbearable trauma and pain.

But in the moment that wish was uttered, I suddenly

realized that if it wasn't for Adolf Hitler, I would not be in this body, in this place at this time. It was because of him and the destruction perpetrated by his followers that my mother and father eventually met in London as refugees. And their meeting and marriage produced me.

The magic wand that I wished could annihilate that psychopathic madman would destroy me, too. My very existence utterly depended upon on this person and the insanity that surrounded him. Furthermore, all the goodness and the miracles of my life and all the wonderful things accomplished by that goodness would vanish with him.

Who was I to say that the existence of this person was unnecessary or unwanted?

I realized in that moment that I was not qualified to judge good from bad, or wrong from right. For years I thought that war was simply an atrocity. Now I have to accept, with Humility, that it was also the reason for my existence.

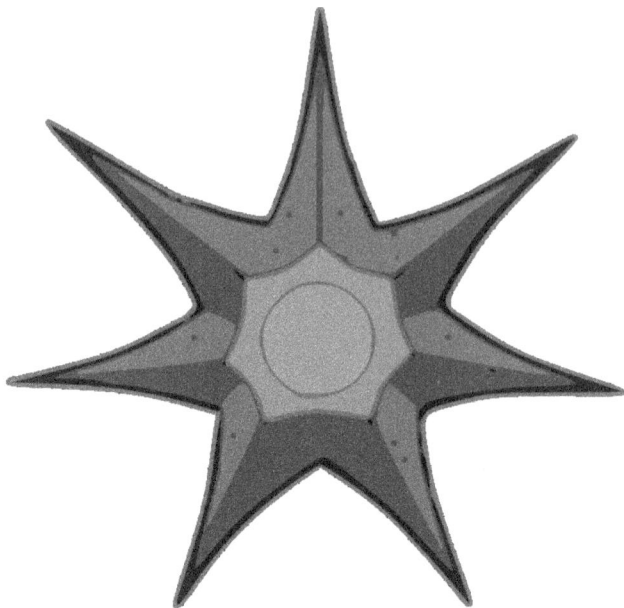

THE THIRD GRANDFATHER TEACHING
COURAGE

Courage is commonly seen as a dynamic energy that we hopefully can access to overcome pain and discomfort to be able to accomplish something of importance to us. And yet in the nature of the life that surrounds us in the trees, streams, and oceans, Courage is not always about forward moving energy.

Makwaa, the Bear, is thought of as the closest relative to the Human Being. She has the ability to go about on two legs as well as four, and is rarely challenged by other beings of the forest.

Makwaa is said to have knowledge of all the medicinal plants, herbs and fruits. But to get its food and medicines, Makwaa needs to move forward. Those berries aren't going to jump into her mouth on their own. The bees are not going to give up their honey without a fight. Makwaa knows what she needs and with Courage moves forward to ensure her survival.

But in order to have her needs met in a good way, her Courage needs to be balanced with fully realized Honesty and *the confidence of Humility. She needs that honey to survive and in fact, deserves it.*

It must be noted that fierceness is not Courage. In humans, fierceness is often a fear reaction. Better to be bold and courageous than fierce and fearful.

As the seasons turn to winter, Makwaa shows us a type of Courage that is passive. When the winds grow chilly and the days grow shorter, she seeks out her cave to hibernate. If she didn't do that, she would surely die because she would not have enough stored energy in her fat to survive being awake and active during the barren winter with nothing to eat. But waking up in the Spring to a new and fruitful world isn't guaranteed for her either. It takes Courage to enter her cave for the winter and be still, without any assurances that she will survive until Spring arrives.

It takes Courage to have absolute and total trust in the ways of Creation.

Life is made up of things you know and things you hope for. To say that you believe in something is actually communicating that you don't believe it and are only guessing that it might be true. If you have experienced something, you no longer need to believe in it because there it is. Things that are a part of your experience are known, and don't need to be believed in or hoped for. It takes Courage to accept things as they are and to turn away from the balm of wishful thinking and the bitterness of disappointment. Fully embodying Honesty and Humility gives us the gift of Courage to know that what we have now, and what we are experiencing now is provided to us for our eventual healing and happiness. The Medicine of Courage moves us forward into the bee's hive to find the sweet and nourishing honey our spirit yearns for.

Our wounds are numerous, many visible only in our memories of when we first were cruelly inflicted. For many of us, taking another breath is an act of Courage. It is important to understand that taking this breath prepares us for what is to come, making us worthy of another minute or two of life. We cannot continue in our bodies without that next breath. And we cannot learn what we need to learn without our bodies. Our spirit is necessarily ensconced in this bag of flesh and bones in the same way Makwaa commits her body deep into the bones and flesh of the Earth. Courageous trust in Creation is the only way we can emerge as whole and vibrant spirits when the deep work that we are called to do for ourselves and the generations to come is complete.

In this way, we are all called to be warriors. We become those who are the last to pick up a weapon, and the first to lay them down. We become worthy of the air we breathe, the same air that is the unconditional gift from Creation that we can't live without for more than a minute or two. As warriors, we become who we are destined to be; that Grandfather or Grandmother sitting at the fire so many generations ago.

It takes Courage to taste fear and deliberately not make a move. It takes Courage to dispense with beliefs and just know. It takes Courage to trust.

A Teaching of the West

The West provides the signal that the day with its light and warmth is ending, and that darkness is approaching. It takes Courage to hold fast to the promise that the light will return, and the dark cold will give way to the warmth of the returning Sun.

The West also teaches us that although light is fading for us, somewhere else the light is returning for our relatives far away from us. We know that by our giving up the warmth of the Sun to the West, others on the other side of our planet can enjoy the warmth, beauty and promise of a new day. In this way, the Circle of Life is complete and never ending. In this way, the Courage of our sacrifice ensures Life.

Often courage only comes when all our other options are exhausted.

Tarnica is a mountain found in south-eastern Poland, the highest peak of the Polish Bieszczady Mountains, close to the borders of the Ukraine and Slovakia. It's a wild place, having been depopulated after the Second World War. It is now home to wolves, bears and Polish bison that live in the primeval Carpathian forest.

On my first pilgrimage to my ancestral homeland I hoped to find and connect with the Spirits of the Wild that my ancient forebears had surely communicated with. Under a sunny blue sky, what had been an image and a dot on a map was now the looming reality of the mountain as I made my way on foot to the trail head at the tiny village of Wołosate. A pair of golden eagles trailed me as I walked down roads that saw much bloodshed between Communist and insurgent forces long after the Nazis were defeated. I felt and heard the spirits of the dead as I walked past the green overgrown ditches and valleys.

Finally, I turned onto the trail leading up out of the valley. It was a balmy Spring day when I began my ascent, threading through the dark moss-grown forest. But beyond the tree line there was mounting snow. The golden eagles who had been trailing me on the narrow country road left me to the care of the coal-black ravens that squawked and tumbled in the air all about the rocky, snow-covered peak a thousand feet above me. In the snow I could see the tracks of bison and could imagine the howling of the wolves that haunted generations of Slavic children. Baba Jaga, the iconic Polish witch who gnawed on the bones of her victims in her dark little hut, could easily feel at home here.

My clothes were now becoming soaked by the wet, cold snow that was knee deep as I made my way up the narrow footpath that spiraled up the conical peak. Yes, I was a fool to be so ill-prepared for this trek, but my desire to see this part of my journey through was overwhelming. The freezing wind that whipped around me hardly mattered as I climbed the last few meters to the peak.

What an incredible view! I could look down into deep green valleys of the Ukraine where Spring was blossoming far below me. To the south and east rose up mountain top after mountain top of the Northern Carpathian Mountain Range that eventually ended at the Black Sea a thousand miles to the South. And to the North one of the great forests of Eastern Europe spread before me to the far horizon. A tall iron crucifix was planted at the very peak of the mountain, sheltering the humble wooden cross that the future Pope John Paul II carried there in his younger days. All about me I could see was the perennial wilderness of this magnificent forgotten corner of the world.

I was entranced with this wild vista, but the cold wind and my wet clothes were reminding me that I needed to go. The sun was beginning to get lower on the Western horizon as I made my way down the icy trail to the bottom of the summit. The topographical map I had of the area showed that there was a second trail that looked like a more direct route westward across a ridge of the mountain down to the forest. Hopefully there was a footpath that I could take back to the village where I was lodging. Because it was now getting later in the afternoon, and I had meager provisions and not enough warm clothing, I decided to take that route.

As I set out it became obvious that this was not a well trodden path. It was icy and treacherously uneven, and the ridge became narrower as it went along. The wind was now getting fierce, blowing across the ridge coming up from the valley on one side and down like a freight train into the deep valley on the other side. The icy mists and blowing snow raced across my trail like galloping spirits that would have *liked nothing better than to blow me off the mountain into the wilderness hundreds of feet below where my body might not be discovered for months if at all. I realized that I had made yet another potentially fatal error, besides my poor gear and meager provisions. I had told no one of my plans. I was just some anonymous American who had a cheap room in a rundown backwoods hostel, and no one had any idea where I was and no one was expecting to hear from me until I returned home. If anything would happen to me it would be days if not weeks before anyone noticed my absence. I was completely and utterly on my own. If I got into trouble, being rescued alive was just not going to happen.*

The map showed that the trail I was following ran in a straight line westward, but there was an abrupt 50-meter drop in elevation after following the ridge for 2 kilometers. I reasoned that surely there must be some safe traverse that managed the descent.

I slogged on through the wind and snow, my shoes now completely soaked as the Sun got closer and closer to the western horizon. Finally, after battling the wind and blinding snow for an hour and a half, I came to a cliff, the one that was shown on my map. But I could not see any path down the rubble of snow-covered boulders and the sun was now nearing the treetops of the forest that I was trying to get to.

My heart froze in fear. I knew that back-tracking to the summit, finding the trail back to Wołosate and then hiking the 5 miles back to my hostel would take four or more hours. There was no doubt that I would succumb to hyperthermia along the way only to be discovered days from now. Turning back was certain death.

From my precipice I could make out the faint outline of a path that ran from the bottom of the cliff to the edge of the forest about a kilometer away, but I saw no way down. I could try to follow the cliff edge hoping to find a trail but that could take hours in rough terrain and it was almost certain that the freezing cold would claim me first.

Wet and shivering, I realized that I needed to get to that path and the forest as quickly as possible. To my left there was one part of the cliff where there had been a landslide that was not as steep but climbing down with my frozen fingers and feet would not be possible. And with all the snow cover, I had no idea where to go and what I could hold on to if I tried to climb down.

I had one choice left. To jump! Yes, I could break my neck or my leg on a hidden boulder, but all my alternatives had certain death awaiting me. I reasoned that if the worst happened, shock and unconsciousness would quickly overtake me, which seemed to me preferable to slowly freezing to death, shelterless, in the howling wind. But, if by some miracle, I survived the jump, then I would certainly make it to my warm room and some food within the hour.

I closed my eyes, prayed that my Higher Power's will for me was to survive, hugged my chest, took a deep breath, and opened my eyes again to find a likely landing spot.

And I jumped.

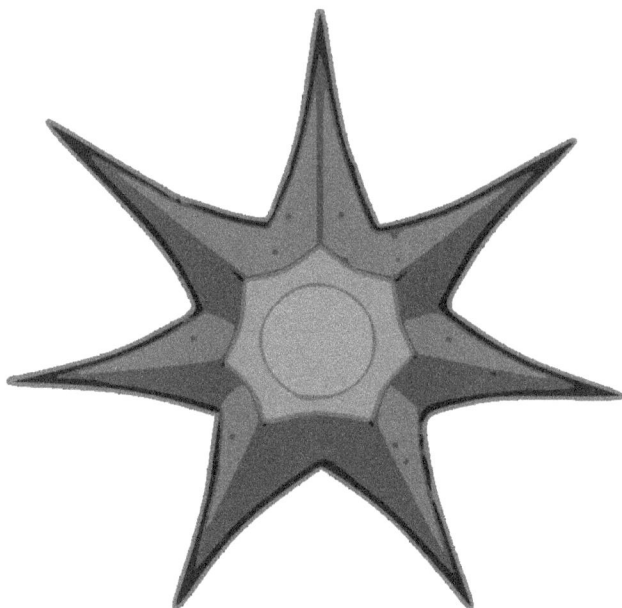

THE FOURTH GRANDFATHER TEACHING

RESPECT

---

*T*here's a lot going on. Everything around us is constantly growing, dying, or breaking down. There is no end to this, and it's impossible to take it all in. So to make things more energetically digestible, we create psychic and perceptual shortcuts. However, there is a great danger here.

Human beings have become very adept at overreaching. Our cleverness creates the illusion that we can do anything, survive anything, and that we can live with impunity outside the boundary of Creation. Much like young children, we have become certain that the entire universe revolves around us and our needs and is subject to our whims and desires. This is immature and disrespectful and is evidence of a lack of understanding of the Natural Law that rules us all.

Without a basic Respect for Life, nothing positive or lasting can come about for us or for the generations to follow.

True Respect cannot be imposed and it cannot be learned. It can only blossom in our hearts when we fully accept and act on the first three Grandfather Teachings of Honesty, Humility,

---

and Courage.

Maengun, the Wolf, survives and thrives in hugely diverse environments from the Sonoran Desert to the High Arctic. In order to survive, Maengun must live the Teachings of Respect. To fully embody these Teachings, he must first see his environment with clear Honesty, or else his survival decisions will doom him and his family. This Honesty enables him to be Humble in a good and constructive way by acknowledging both his abilities and limitations. The Medicine of Courage then helps him to move forward to face the unknown that is often wrapped in harsh reality.

Finally, the Medicine of Respect that flows from those three Teachings prevents him from overreaching or trying to dominate forces far more powerful than he. Embodying the Medicine of Respect, Maengun can live in balance with himself and the environment that can both nourish him and his family or kill him.

Wise Elders have traveled this road of Life and know it as well as a wolf knows the tracks of the caribou through the snow in the wilderness. Sitting in the North of the Medicine Wheel, the Elders clearly see how the experiences of their lives interact, beginning in the East as an infant, and continuing through the South as a youth and the West as an adult, making them who they are in the North as Elders. They see this not only for themselves, but they see their story reflected in the lives of those around them. They understand that they have a choice; to be jealous of experiences they did not have or to embrace their relations and their relations' experiences with Respect, knowing that their relations' stories are also their story.

Life in this world is not a take-it-or-leave-it proposition. One cannot walk away from the consequences of one's actions. You might not feel them immediately or directly, but there are always consequences and they will affect you and those close to you without fail.

And conversely, everything we experience during our Earth Walk is enormously influenced by the prior actions taken by others.

When we look back on our life's journey, we will see that there has not been one instant when someone simply appeared out of the blue lacking a history of their own. Everyone and everything have a story. And each has left a trail of experience whose origins have absolutely nothing to do with us, but at the same time have a profound effect on our life and experiences.

The journey of the Grandfather Teachings around the

Medicine Wheel shows us how our lives can be consciously ordered to obtain the highest form of satisfaction in living well. We begin with Honesty in the East, the direction of new light and clarity. We then travel with the Sun to the South, where our values are nurtured in the safety of Humility. It is then that we can stand up for ourselves in a good way in the West with the Courage of a bear.

Finally, it all comes together in the North as these attributes allow Respect for our environment and our relations to come forth, for our survival and the survival of the generations.

A Teaching of the North

The North is the other end of the great axis around which our Earth spins, centering us around the gifts and knowledge of a life well lived.

It is no accident that the Medicines of Humility and Respect face each other across the Medicine Wheel. Both are the constants that hold the axis of our lives steady.

Everything matters and thus deserves our respect.

Years ago, early on this journey, I stood next to my old Chevy pick-up truck and realized that every bit of it came from this Earth. All the steel was once iron ore. All the plastic was once crude oil hidden beneath the Earth's crust. All the glass was once silica, like the sand we find at the shore of the ocean. There was nothing on that Chevy that came from anywhere but this Earth.

Standing there, under the stars with one foot on the bumper, I began to travel backwards in time in my mind's eye, tracing the origins of this bumper, first to the factory where it was installed on the chassis of this truck, and then to the gigantic stamping machine that formed it with a tremendous bang out of a sheet of steel. I followed my bumper back to the foundry where molten metal was formed into billets and then sheets, keeping track of the specific atoms and molecules of iron and chrome that made up the bumper of the truck that I was leaning on.

I kept following those atoms and molecules backwards in time through the smelter that separated them from the rocks and rubble that held them as ore, backwards on the specific truck and barge or train car that transported those specific rocks from the pits that they were dug out of. I saw the shovels and machines tearing at the Earth, dislodging those rocks that contained the atoms and molecules that eventually made up my bumper, rocks that spent countless millennia in the peaceful dark of the folds of this Earth.

And, still following my atoms and molecules, I saw our Earth being miraculously formed out of bits of material thrown out by our young Sun utilizing the magic of gravity and inertia. And traveling even further back in time I saw this amazing conglomeration of energy and matter that was to be our Sun, pregnant with the atoms that were destined to be the bumper on the truck that I was resting my foot on. And not only that, all the atoms of all the machines and human hands that touched, moved, formed and installed this bumper were there in that Sun as well.

Nothing was missed. It was all there. Everything.

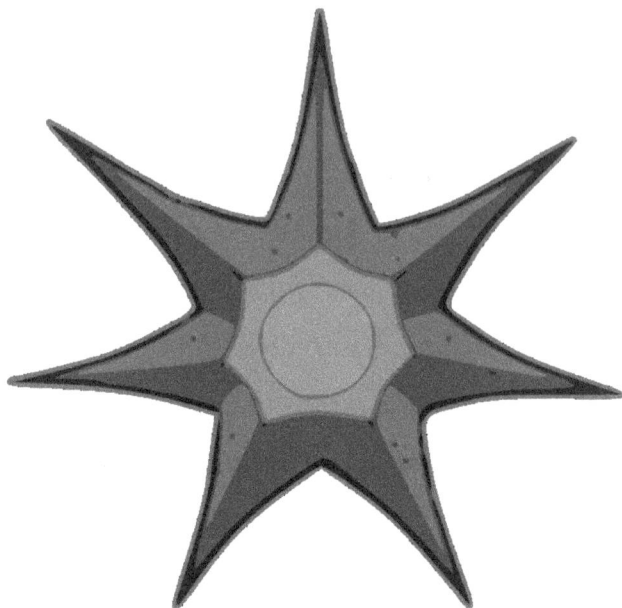

THE FIFTH GRANDFATHER TEACHING

GENEROSITY

---

*S*omehow humans developed the notion that they could predict the future. But with that imagined knowledge comes fear, riding like a ghost on a spectral horse, poisoning our innate longing for survival. Every microbe, plant, and fleshy being is bent on surviving. This programming is one of the great Mysteries.

Go out and look up at the sky on a clear night. Every star that you see has another star beyond it. And the stars that you cannot see with your eyes alone have more stars and galaxies, and universes behind them. Even the very furthest gaseous accumulation of dust and energy has something just on the other side of it. We might not know what that something is, but that doesn't mean it isn't there. Of course, it is. That is the meaning of infinity. There is no end to it.

When we look up at the night sky, we literally see all that is, which includes all that ever was in what we perceive as the past and all that will ever be. Physicists have expressed this truth as the Law of Conservation of Mass. Matter and energies cannot just disappear. They are simply transformed.

Our physical experience of the present is simply light, electrical and vibrational energy, thickened into a form that we can perceive in this moment before it is transformed into what we call the past. What we experience as the past is simply that same light, electrical, and vibrational energy being released into the Infinite, much like a broadcast radio signal traveling outward at the speed of light.

As we look up into the face of Infinity with clarity, we begin to understand that everything already exists. There are no such things as possibilities. In an infinite universe, nothing needs to be possible because everything already exists. Every speck of light from every birthday candle you ever blew out is somehow, impossibly, still traveling outward towards that last star and beyond. And the hot energy of the spark that will ignite the next candle already resides in some match in some box somewhere on the planet.

We are accustomed to see Generosity in the act of giving, but paradoxically there is Generosity in receiving as well. To be able to receive generously, we need to know who we are and where we are on our life's journey.

With humility we need to honestly know our true and proper place among all that is. We need courage to overcome our fears of unworthiness, and we need to respect the necessity of being given to by another. Honesty, Humility, Courage, and Respect need to be within us as we go forth as open, loving, effective participants in the Life around us.

The physical realm in which we now abide is ruled by duality. Every up need a down to exist. There can be no darkness without light. Insides need outsides to be inside of. There is nothing wrong with this. This is how babies learn to negotiate the world around them, and to gain the physical and cognitive maturity that is required to proceed on their Earth Walk. There's a lesson to be learned in every bruise, a strength that is gained in every stumble.

But duality is very limited and soon loses its usefulness as a tool for spiritual and physical maturation. Perpetually falling on your diapered bottom and not developing the ability to walk on your own is no path to a happy life.

Dualistic perception makes no sense when confronted with the physical reality of the infinite Universe. Unfortunately, Infinity scares the willies out of us clever monkeys, and so we have collectively decided that it is Infinity that doesn't make sense (regardless of its physical reality), and have done all we can to shore up dualism as best we can.

Paradox is not welcomed. Holding two disparate concepts as true in the same instance is just too much. However, unless *we can embrace paradox, and somehow suspend our confusion, we will always wonder why our entire wonderful intellectual constructs and beliefs always end up as such disasters.*

That is why receiving with Generosity is a great gift that we can give to our people. By embodying this small paradox, we humbly demonstrate how receiving as well as giving with Generosity completes the Sacred Circle of Life. We acknowledge and honor the Infinite with every small act of receiving.

This Teaching of Generosity is the beginning of our new relationship with All That Is. If we are truly living generously, then we no longer have the ability to judge others as evil or wrong. How could they be in an infinite Universe? What we might have called aberrant behavior, we can now see as a need for teaching or a need for healing.

A Teaching of the Above

Look up!

The Sky above is filled with treasures for our delight and inspiration. The denizens of the Sky World not only witness all that has transpired but are also the repository of all the vibrations of all our actions and their consequences.

Above us is a magnificent treasure trove of Life, sparkling with the diamond light of the infinite stars and galaxies, and the light of the campfires of our Ancestors!

We might be small compared the vastness of the physical Universe, but our hearts and spirits are huge, and more than enough.

Generosity is our birthright, and the only thing that keeps our lives in balance.

When I get really afraid, I experience the kind of fear that locks me up and keeps me from any creative ideas and separates me from the world around me.

You know that kind of fear? It's that eddy of suffocating emotion where you just go round and round endlessly circling about whatever it is that is so frightening.

It was yet another night of drinking and bickering. Sometimes these would end in 'make-up sex', but not tonight. Things got out of hand. Words that should have never passed our lips were said. The horror and noise grew until one of us had enough and walked out the door, even though we had, in our sober moments, solemnly swore that neither one of us would ever leave the other in anger.

It didn't happen that night. The pressure to be right and righteous was too great. We had one or more too many drinks, and the barbarity of alcohol ruled.

The door slammed and I watched her tear off down the driveway in a cloud of dust. I turned from the window and thought, "This is it. It's over." It wasn't that my marriage was over. No, I meant that my life was done, finished, kaput. I *had enough. Too many tears had been shed, scorched by too many memories of failed dreams, unrealized hopes, and squandered gifts. I had enough of living.*

The month before, I had bought a .45 semi-automatic handgun and a box of ammunition. Each bullet felt heavy in my hand, large and lethal. We lived on a rural Ohio farmstead, and my excuse was that we needed some form of protection.

I kept it, loaded, in the glove box of my truck and sometimes at night I would go out a get it just to feel the weight of it in my hand. And sometimes, just because I was curious how it would feel, I would put the barrel to my temple or sometimes in my mouth, pressed to the roof of my mouth. I was very careful to be sure that the safety was on, and that there wasn't a round in the chamber. After all, it was just a harmless investigation.

But this night was different. I knew that I could put a bullet in the chamber, take the safety off, put the gun to my head and pull the trigger, and I knew that I had to. I was well acquainted with all the proscriptions against taking my life, from the eternal damnation taught by my Catholic upbringing, to the horrible karma described by the Vedic teachings that I was now beginning to embrace. I fully understood the horrific consequences of what I was about to do and yet the pain of my life felt so great that I was willing to cross that line just so that I could be relieved of the immense suffering I felt in that moment.

I felt calm and fully resolved as I rose out of my chair so that I could get the gun.

In that moment, as clearly as if someone was standing right behind me, I heard a man say "Don't!" I turned but there was no one there. Of course. I was the only one in the house and our closest neighbor was a quarter mile away. Again, I heard the voice say, "Don't!" except louder and more vehemently.

Stunned and confused I sat back down in my chair. "How could this be?" I wondered. There was no doubt that there was a voice in the room, but the room was empty. As I recovered from my shock, I slowly came to the realization that someone somewhere loved me so much that they made sure I heard them. What a difficult and huge effort that must have been to send me that message in a way that I could hear it through my pain and drunkenness. In fact, I was so startled that I no longer felt drunk. The effects of the alcohol had completely lifted, and I was totally sober as I sat there, taking this realization in.

Someone out there loved me. I knew that for sure. They

loved me so much that they did everything they could to keep me from destroying myself. I could not ignore that. I could not just walk away from them and shoot myself anyway. I couldn't do it then, or ever.

For you see, suicide was always my trump card. As long as I had my hand on the switch of my life, I could bear unimaginable pain because I knew that when it would get too great, I could pull the switch and the pain would be gone. Or so I reasoned. The ability to extinguish myself whenever I wanted was within my power. I had that total control of my life. What I didn't realize was that power made my life worse and progressively more chaotic, because I did not exercise any caution or control over my emotional life. I didn't have to as long as I had my hand on the switch, or in this case my finger on the trigger. What I didn't see was that I had doomed myself and that suicide was the inevitable end of my life. The riches of life that should have been mine would never be.

In the instant that I heard that voice say, "Don't", I knew I couldn't, and I could feel my trump card slowly slip away. Relief and fear were what I felt that night. But today, 30 years later, immense gratitude fills me when I think back on that night. Life did not become instantly better. In fact, in many ways it became more difficult for a time. I still drank and my wife and I still fought. But far outweighing the trials and tribulations that came my way were the immense blessings and joys and experiences that I never would have had if that voice had not come to me and if I had not listened.

All thoughts of suicide as an option were lifted that night. However, it took some time for something else to trickle in to replace it.

That something else is my connection with a Power greater than myself. Some might call it prayer, but there is more than supplication in my conversations with that Power. There are times when I am gloriously pissed off at God, and have no reservation going nose-to-nose with He, She, or It telling them exactly how I feel about them in the most graphic language I can concoct in that moment.

But no matter what gets thrown my way, I will never forget that night and once again my gratitude for the new life that began in that moment overwhelms whatever anger and frustration that might be dancing in front of me today.

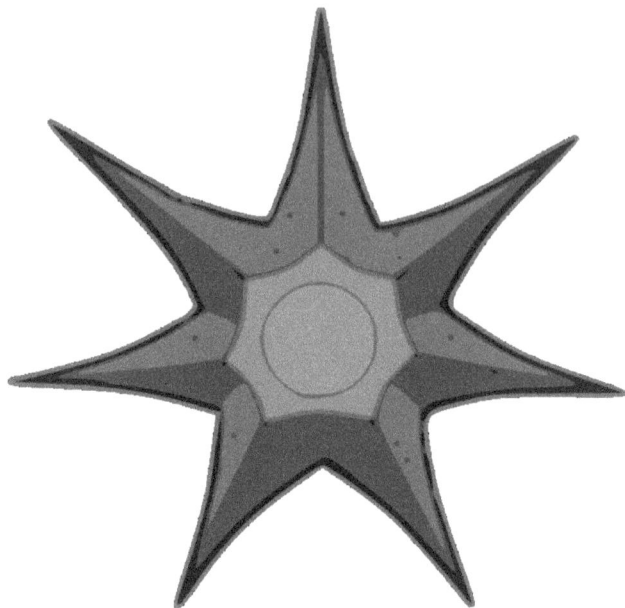

THE SIXTH GRANDFATHER TEACHING

WISDOM

Wisdom has become monetized. 'Spiritual Teachers' are out there by the millions (really) trying to pay their rent (or mortgages). They dress up in flamboyant clothing, groom their shiny, curly hair, and make sure that they smell nice and exotic. They prey on the vulnerable, unhappy mass of humans with their snake oil 'wisdom'.

Here's the truth. Wisdom is innate in every one of us. When watered and nurtured by our Honesty, Humility, Courage, Respect and Generosity, Wisdom blossoms forth like a seed that we have long carried in our hearts and minds.

Wisdom is not acquired. It is not a commodity. It cannot be sold or bartered. Wisdom does not require intelligence or knowledge. Wisdom is the gift of having lived.

Wisdom is not limited to just the two-legged creatures either. Quiet, profound Wisdom resides in the Trees and the Stone People and the Waters.

The deepest Wisdom is whispered, not trumpeted. There is a vital reason for this. It is often misunderstood that Wisdom *is a tool for teaching. But how can anyone teach what already resides within? The only reason some might seem unwise is that their spirit is so tightly shut that no light can penetrate, like a room with no windows. The only thing another's Wisdom can do is provide light in dark places so that the gifts of Life can be seen... if the eyes of the Spirit are willing to open.*

Imagine that we are all traveling in a long train of carriages. We can only guess what is moving this train forward, and there is nothing to be done except take care of ourselves and be nice to the people next to us, if we choose. Or we can ignore everything and just enjoy the beauty of the landscape we are traveling through.

Occasionally, someone in the carriage will stand up and shout: "I am wise! Listen to me!" With great passion, they will tell the rest of us that they know what is moving this train, and where this train is heading. And because they think they know these things, they feel the need to be in charge if only for our own good. Oddly, it seems that they want us to pay attention only to them, ignoring everything else including the spectacular scenery rolling by. If they convince enough people, tensions can arise, distracting the rest of us from the beauty that is passing by our windows at every moment.

In the meantime, the passing scenery becomes ever more colorful and beautiful regardless of who is paying attention to it.

In the Old Testament it is written, "So God created man in his own image..." (Genesis 1:27). The tragic mistake is that humans invariably get this wrong and end up trying to worship a God that is made in man's image. A lot of wars, death and suffering could have been avoided if certain people could have kept this one detail straight.

Creating God in man's own image is far more responsibility than we are designed to cope with. It's an unnecessary, useless, and stupid thing to try to do. If any one of us was in total control of Life, and the Universe, it would all collapse in a nanosecond. All the intricate, interdependent mechanisms of Life are way beyond any human's ability to keep in balance.

Declaring that you are among the Wise is just about the stupidest thing a human can do.

The smartest thing to do is to let the mystery of life be God, and just sit back and enjoy the ride. There are always going to be scuffles in the aisles, and sometimes they need our attention. But don't forget to enjoy the scenery passing by. Our destination is unknown, but the truth and beauty of living should not be ignored.

A Teaching from our Mother

Our Mother Earth provides everything that we need to sustain and nourish us.

A tree does not bear fruit in the winter for it to uselessly wither and die. Water never stops flowing from the sky, finding its way into the streams of our valleys, through the veins of our bodies and the bodies of all the plant life to finally arrive at the ocean, only to be lifted up, once again purified, into the sky, in a perfect continuity of cleansing and refreshment.

This is the innate wisdom of our Mother Earth. Nothing comes before its time and all is nurtured, refreshed and renewed for all of Her children.

Allowing the seeds of yours and others to grow to wholeness in their own time and way is Wisdom. Trust that it will blossom within you in its own time and place like the wondrous wildflowers that our Mother Earth provides for us with in the right places at the right moments. Then the words from your mouth which sound so ordinary in your ears will shed an extraordinary light into the dark places of those you love.

Wisdom is the silent and patient architect of our lives.

I was living in Maine soon after leaving a very high paying senior executive position in another state. Unfortunately, the economy had suddenly plunged into a deep recession and I couldn't find a job commensurate with the prestige and salary level I had previously enjoyed. All the doors that should have been open to me were closed tight.

Months and then years went by. My wife and I moved from one state to another. I was compelled to take jobs selling life insurance, moving furniture, cleaning horse stalls and even delivering newspapers to put food on the table.

At one point I took a job as a part-time clerk in a hardware store in a small Midwestern town. The work was enjoyable enough and steady, but it was unbelievable to me that the best I could do was working for less than a fifth of what I was used to making just two years before. I felt pretty despondent at what seemed like the end of the line for me.

But the funny thing was, while I was working as a clerk in that store, a contractor came in who was looking for some extra help in his business. I didn't know anything about his work but he really needed someone to help for a short bit of time, so I agreed. Within a year I ended up running his business for him. And with the skills that I learned from him, I eventually began my own business, and in the thirty some years later, I've earned literally millions of dollars, traveled the world, got sober, found my spiritual bearings, and ended up owning a home in a beautiful tropical paradise.

All this came from being a part-time clerk in a small Midwestern hardware store when I was down and out. It showed me that you never know what is fortunate or unfortunate in life. The end of one line is just the beginning of another.

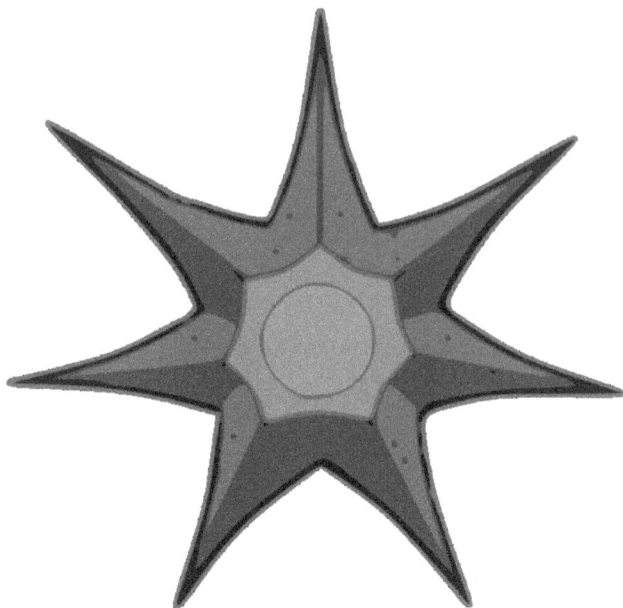

THE SEVENTH GRANDFATHER TEACHING

LOVE

---

*W*e've all seen the research. Babies who are loved and held do much better than babies who are never touched. So there is no doubt that we need this Love thing. But, here we go again. Pretty quickly, humans discovered that love can make you lots of money, if you play it right.

Atoms are clumps of neutrons and protons that have tiny little electrons orbiting around them. And these atoms clump together making stuff like liquids, solids and gases. Different atoms clump together and make more stuff like molecules, which make proteins and such. Everything around us is made this way; clumps of this little stuff.

How this works has been the subject of much conjecture to the point that we actually think we know the ins and outs of all this clumping. Newtonian Physics, Laws of Thermodynamics, and so on do a very good job of describing how all of this works, but never answer the question, "Why?"

We could suppose that all this clumping is simply arbitrary, and "Why?" would then become a very stupid and irrelevant *question.*

But consider this: If the infinite Universe was arbitrary, then why such a stringent adherence to what we call the Laws of Physics? How come the glass of water that you are bringing to your lips stays water? If this were a truly arbitrarily ordered existence, then that sweet tasting water could suddenly become deadly battery acid, but it doesn't. The gravity that we depend on to keep things together is remarkably consistent on every square inch of this planet. Why is that?

Arbitrary conditions by their nature are inconsistent, and this inconsistency begets chaos. In a chaotic universe, gravity would come and go. Solids would become liquid for no reason. The things that we depend on for our existence moment by moment, like air and water, could turn into substances that poison us in an instant. Life could not be possible at any level.

The ordering of the physical world that we experience is not chaotic. Air is always air, and a carrot is always a carrot. We don't have to worry about it. Indeed, our world is so consistently ordered for our survival that we don't even need to think about the most basic things that are keeping us alive from one minute to the next. We breathe and take in life-giving air without a thought. Everything that we touch, eat, and use originates from the Earth that we walk upon. We raise our glasses to our lips and drink water without a thought of the miracles of cleansing that water has for us. The ball of fire that we call the Sun arrives every day, showering us with a light and warmth that we cannot do without.

Without supplication or sacrifice, we are surrounded by the things that we need to continue living.

This cannot be arbitrary. There is an order to things, and order can only come from conscious action. Conscious action can only come from something being consciously acted upon. Which leads us to the inevitable conclusion that there is some mysterious and conscious something or other that holds our physical reality consistent and dependable.

We are provided for mysteriously. And this mysterious consciousness has at its core Unconditional Love. It simply cannot be otherwise. The alternative is chaos, and if this were to ever be a chaotic universe it would disappear in a nanosecond. How could anything go on, ever arbitrarily shifting and changing?

There is no doubt. Everything we need is lovingly and consistently provided for.

This is the Medicine of the Seventh Grandfather:

Unconditional Love. All are welcome to these gifts. It's true that we might deny them, and withhold them from one another, but the gifts of Life are always there. We might spoil and pollute them to the point of harming ourselves, but that is a choice that we have made. The gifts that come from that mysterious loving entity arrive on our doorstep pure and available. The consistency and unconditionality of these life sustaining gifts are ample evidence of a loving provider.

Unconditional Love is the glue that holds everything together. That is what fills the spaces between all the tiny particles whizzing around that make up our world.

If we were able to travel sub-atomically, we would never be able to experience separation between the water and the glass. We would be traversing the universe in the space between the electrons, neutrons, and protons and could never differentiate the glass from the water, or the air and our bodies. In this way, we are all together one substance, and that substance has a loving and consistent core.

A Teaching of Love

Love is the glue of our existence, no matter what stories we make up about it.

All the statues, effigies, trinkets and books are just small childish attempts to see what can't be fully seen and to understand what we can't fully know. Infinity is a fact of life, and unknowable. All we really know is what we can touch, taste, smell, feel, hear and see.

Let that be enough. To consciously touch the skin of Infinity is our doorway to the understanding that we all crave.

And don't forget your gratitude. Always say 'please' and 'thank you' for the life you have. Remember, Love loves love.

Love cannot be love unless it is unconditional.

In western Massachusetts, between the Connecticut River and the Quabbin Reservoir, there is a small 1,100 foot mountain called Mount Mineral. It is a wild place with mineral springs, pine groves, swamps and forest, and a mysterious man-made cave of unknown origins. At the top of the mountain are four small rustic cabins and a gathering hall that make up a retreat center called Temenos. The unique feature of this center is that there are no modern conveniences such as electricity or plumbing. Water is drawn from a well, as it was 150 years ago. It is uniquely quiet and separate from any of the commotion of the modern world. The view from the west facing cliffs extends to Mount Graylock near the New York state line over 55 miles away and is uncluttered with any power lines, roads or houses.

This was where I spent many hours and days meditating and praying, and where the whispers of life could be heard in the silence. When my soul ached for peace, and my heart begged for answers, this is where I would go to find solace.

One Spring day, when the leaves of the trees were just beginning to bud, I parked my truck at the foot of the long trail that led up to the retreat center. Before beginning my climb, I stopped and paid my respects to the spirits that I knew were inhabiting the little cave built into the side of hill.

I don't remember the particular reason for my being there that day but walking the old logging road that wound its way through the swamps and forest was how the troubles of my soul slowly began to unwind. However, on this day, as I began my walking meditation, I noticed that the underbrush on the side of the road was somehow disturbed. I stepped off of the path and saw that someone had laid a thin telephone cable following the road, and it was obvious that this cable started at some pole along the road near the cave, and continued all the way up to the retreat center. The further I walked up the old road the more disturbed I became. Where there had been once no connection to the outside world in any way, there was now a thin copper wire that connected the chaos that I needed to leave behind, into the very heart of this last place of quiet and solitude. The violation of this sanctuary felt like a rape, and I became more furious as I made my way up.

I finally turned onto the path to the cliffs, hoping that at least there I could find some peace for my now extremely agitated spirit. However, when I got there, I found that someone had taken a chainsaw and literally shaved down all the trees that had grown up on and below the cliffs, ostensibly *to improve the view. Seeing all the litter and branches of all those precious trees was too much for me.*

And I cried out! "How could this happen? How could you, the spirit guardians of this holy place, allow this? Aren't you stronger than this evil? How could you let this happen?" I felt shattered and betrayed. This beautiful, vibrant, wild place had been decimated by the hand of some callous humans blinded by their self-interest.

Suddenly I heard a small clear voice. "It's true," the voice said softly. "We allowed this to happen. Yes, we are strong, strong enough to stop this. But we love you. We love all of you unconditionally. That means if you feel the need to do something even if it is this harmful and degrading, we will not stand in your way. Not because we are too weak to forestall it, but because in fact we are strong. Our unconditional love for you could never allow us to stand in the way of something that you have decided is necessary for your happiness even if it is misdirected. But we know, and you must know, that we are stronger than that. The peace that you are seeking can never be destroyed, except by your own hand. And when you are done, when the lessons you have called to yourself have been learned, we will return this place to the way it was meant to be."

It's true. On any sidewalk in any city you will find a soft blade of grass pushing through the hard concrete. A road that is no longer used very quickly becomes overgrown, allowing saplings and wildflowers to once again flourish. There is nothing that can stop life from finally reclaiming its own. Even the most desolate desert is teeming with insects and lizards seeming to exist on nothing. And there they are, unstoppable.

That small voice told me, "Don't be fooled by our actions or seeming lack of action. All that we do is informed by the unconditional love we have for you humans. We are not weak. We are strong enough to be patient for you to run the course of your trials and errors. And when you are done, we will make ourselves known, because we have never left."

Jerzy M. Kokurewicz

CHOICES

t is at this time that the light skinned race will be given a choice between two roads. If they choose the right road, then the Seventh Fire will light the Eighth and final Fire, an eternal fire of peace, love, brotherhood and sisterhood. If the light skinned race makes the wrong choice of roads, then the destruction which they brought with them in coming to this country will come back at them and cause much suffering and death to all the Earth's people." <u>From The Mishomis Book - The Voice of the Ojibway, by Eddie Benton-Banai.</u>[1]

You have a choice to make, and it isn't an easy one.

Making a declaration of choice is not choosing. Declaring an intention simply means that you aren't doing it now. Now is the only reality we have.

Our heads are filled with the voices of lawyers, street magicians and other con artists, and any choices that come from our intellect are subject to the machinations of our busy monkey minds. Decisions from that quarter are unreliable at best, and downright devious with self-serving interests trumping all else, including our happiness.

Our minds come up with wonderful questions but lousy

answers. All we really have is our hearts. Our poor, abused, wounded hearts.

But the good news is that the Journey of Healing is also the Journey of Wisdom and Happiness. It's worth taking.

These Teachings can be your road map. Use these Teachings to heal. Let the Grandfathers touch you through these words. And before you know it, the right choice will be made for you.

EMBODIMENT

*L*ife lessons cannot stay alive in a book. They must be embodied.

And so it must be here.

It's one thing to understand these Grandfather Teachings intellectually but living them requires more than just a mental agreement to them.

There is a choice to be made.

So, if these Teaching resonate at all with you, it is only because you are somehow hearing the ancient beckoning of your distant ancestors. A faint echo in your spirit longs for this.

This is your choice. Listen or turn away.

Jerzy M. Kokurewicz

BEGIN WITH HONESTY

A nd not just truth-telling! Much of what we portray as truth is relative and incomplete. And much of what we call truth-telling is concocted from our own wounded spirits.

The best way to embody a deep sense of Honesty is to identify your values.

What is the best way to do that? It seems backwards, but the clearest way to understand what you value is when it is not present.

Are people who are rude upsetting to you? Then Courtesy and Respect must be some of your values.

Do you get angry when someone lies to you? Perhaps Trustworthiness and Honesty are among your values.

Do you feel pain when a friend turns their back on you? Loyalty could be a value, too.

Go through your day and make a list of what set you off, and what upset you, or stimulated your negative judgment. Next to each one, list what you would have liked to have experienced instead. Boil them down to one word each, and *you have the beginning of your list of values.*

Memorize this list. Have this list in front of you at all times. Take time at the end of every day to see how you did. Repeat, repeat, repeat until you no longer need to think about them. This world would be such a more pleasant place to live in if, when asked, every person knew what they valued and had it right on the tip of their tongues.

Our shortcomings are not who we truly are. For instance, no one really wants to be Greedy. Greed is just a flawed means to achieve happiness that fails not only the greedy one, but all those around him. The same applies to Jealousy, Anger, and all of those negative mind-states that all of us Humans are subject to.

Our values are the only honest reflection of who we are. We are not angry people; we are scared people trying to deflect the pain of our fear. We are not jealous people; we simply are scared that somehow, we will be denied the respect and love that we know we deserve.

*Here is the list of **my** values: Trustworthiness, Loyalty, Helpfulness, Friendliness, Courtesy, Kindness, Obedience, Cheerfulness, Thrift, Bravery, Cleanliness and Reverence. This might sound familiar to some of you because it is the old Scout's Law that I memorized as a Boy Scout 50 years ago.*

That memorization has stood me in good stead for many decades. It gives me a sense of pride that deep in my psyche I know who I really am, even in the darkest days of my life.

Make your list. Write it down a hundred times. Memorize your list like a third grader learning a part in the school play. Repeat it every day. That's all you have to do. That is all the effort that is needed, because as you embody this list you will gradually awaken to the true self you always were, and the other false idea of who you thought you were will silently slip away.

Jerzy M. Kokurewicz

EMBRACE HUMILITY

O nce we achieve that deeper sense of Honesty, and start to believe in who we really are, we begin to see our place in the scheme of things more clearly. We start to understand that Creation is not here to serve us. We are here to serve Creation in a myriad of small ways whether we are conscious of it or not.

There is one destiny that none of us will fail. We are all destined to be food. No matter how we have led our lives, how saintly or desultory our behavior, in the end our bodies will provide sustenance to some worm, microbe, maggot, or crab. This is certain. It will be the smallest of our relations that will gobble us up. This is how we will all inevitably serve Creation no matter what.

Here is an easy way to practice humility. Hold your breath. Do it now! ....

How did you do?

No matter how hard we try, we cannot stop breathing. We have to breathe. Our bodies take over and force us to take that breath, usually within a minute for most of us. We have no control over this.

Our lives utterly depend on the air that we breathe. Our physical needs for food, shelter, transport and so on can only be met by the Earth and all her bounty. Without the cleansing powers of the waters, we would suffocate in our own excrement. And without the life kindling heat and the radiant light of fire, we would stumble around blindly, completely unable to take in the gorgeous beauty that surrounds us.

Take away any one of these vital elements and our lives as we have become accustomed will end within minutes. There is no exception to this fact.

We are utterly dependent on the presence of air, earth, water and fire.

HAVE COURAGE

B efore the Bear can eat the honey, she has to want the honey. How else could she endure the fierce swarm of bees in the hive and the hundreds of painful stings she needs to expose herself to in order to taste the sweetness she longs for.

What is your honey? What is the vision you have of a wonderful, perfect existence for yourself and your world?

You might think that your perfect world would consist of an endless orgy of food, sex and other intoxicating activities, but think carefully. How will that end? How would that version of perfection serve you and the ones who love you? Can all the food in the world fill your endless craving? No. Can all the alcohol and drugs that you could consume bring you to ultimate happiness, or will it eventually cause you to crash and burn, wanting more and more?

If the honey of your choosing can't sustain or satisfy you, what is the point? If chasing after that particular honey will result in chaos and misery for yourself and everyone around you, why would you want to do that?

We have no idea what is going to happen 10 minutes from

now. What will we be thinking? What will be our body postures, or even our emotions 10 minutes from now? We might think we know but in reality, the next moments of our existence are a mystery to us.

Of course, we need structure in our lives, just like we need structures to keep our bodies dry and warm. But those structures, be they family, or careers, or a passionate love affair with either another person or an idea, are not our lives. They are only like the trellis that ivy pulls itself up on to reach ever closer to our beloved Sun.

If we try to inhibit where and how the ivy of our life climbs, we might never know the heights and beauty it could have reached on its own. Of course, we need to show up for our lives. Of course, we want to help it along. But to have a life that is sweet and nourishing we need the ivy of our lives to be built on the structure of our values.

Take this moment and envision the kind of world you would like to live in right now. Be courageous. Don't be discouraged by the doubts and the fears of what you perceive as your shortcomings. Recognize that your diseased thinking will always pull you down. Lift your spirit up to the holy light of the Sun of your soul.

Craft a short sentence that expresses your deepest desire

and hope for your existence. And then write it down. Make it concrete and visible.

This, along with the list of your values, is your trellis. You might change and refine it from time to time, but make this your honey. Make this statement your reason for existing today.

As you allow this statement of your existence to sink deep into your psyche, the Courage to do your part in creating the world you desire will arise naturally within you without any effort. And whatever stings that you might encounter will not stop you from reaching for that sweet honey that will sustain you. And above, all be patient and keep your pruning shears aside for now.

Let the unknown be an equal partner in your life. Let this Great Mystery unfold within your being, and you will find the Courage of the Bear.

Jerzy M. Kokurewicz

RESPECT ALL THAT IS

Why are you reading this?

I *don't mean the intellectual or emotional 'Why?' I'm not interested in your reasons for being here whether it's for yourself or all of humanity.*

The 'Why?' that I'm interested in and the 'Why?' that is the most important and honest is 'How did you come to be reading these words, in this time and in this place?'

How did you find this book? What led you to be sitting in the chair, or airplane, or sleeping bag you are in right now? What happened yesterday that made today possible? And the day before that? And the day before that?

It is in the seemingly mundane answers to these questions that we find the most profound reality. Whose hands touched the chair you are sitting in? Whose hands sorted and packed and unpacked the case of books that held this one? Every one of those hands was attached to a body like yours that has a mind and consciousness like yours, that had ideas and thoughts that came from experiences that in many ways were like yours. All the people that touched your chair and this book through its many phases experienced doubts, and hopes, and fears, and hunger, and delight. Just like you.

There is one thing that we all hunger for, more than love, more than notoriety, more than sex. That thing is Respect. Love cannot exist without Respect. As our awakening progresses, we begin to understand how fundamental Respect is for us.

And if Respect is so fundamental to our wellbeing, then it is so for all the minds and bodies that are attached to all the hands that put our lives together without us knowing it.

So many things have contributed to our lives. So many gifts have come our way. We really have no idea. So many invisible hands built our lives and our furniture and our clothing and our food. Every one of those lives attached to those invisible hands deserves our respect even if it's only because we desire it for ourselves.

When I looked at my old Chevy pick-up truck, I saw that every bit of it came from this Earth. And every bit of that truck was touched, moved and shaped by someone just like me, and by unknown forces that had a part in the creation of the raw materials used.

Take a moment, pausing to think about how your chair came to be. And every morning when you pull on your shirt, or your blouse or your dress, think about all the happy and sad people that touched your clothing before it came to you. And every day, as you settle into your chair to either relax or work, remember the tree or the rock that was shaped and manipulated into this final form that you are now enjoying.

Remembering and not forgetting is the deepest form of Respect that you can bestow on the Universe.

Jerzy M. Kokurewicz

BE INFINITELY GENEROUS

You are the recipient of universal generosity. All the air you need is right here, available to you with no strings attached. The richest, most beautiful person in the world has no more air than you do. Wealth doesn't matter. Power and influence don't matter. Air is all that matters. And we all have it.

Each breath is a kiss of life.

Think of all the human beings you encountered today, each friend, store clerk, and stranger. See them in your mind's eye and smile at them. If there were kind words, remember them. Recall every small sweet gesture, nicety and twinkling eye.

Kindness is the ultimate currency of generosity.

Perhaps today you were not particularly kind to someone. We all have our reasons why we might fall short. But there is always tomorrow and perhaps then you might remember to be kind. But for now, be kind to yourself. Forgive yourself. Be generous to yourself.

Generosity does not mean inappropriate indulgence or giving someone license to disrespect your boundaries. If *today you experienced someone's disrespect, at least from this distance of time and space from that person, be kind, even if you are still angry. Perhaps your anger can't be helped, but you can always find a way to be kind. You can be generous with your kindness.*

The practice of generosity in your mind is accumulative. The more you access generosity in your imagination, the more it will manifest in your daily living.

Remember, you don't depend on other's reciprocity of kindness to survive today because you have all the air you need. In this very moment you have everything you need to go on for another minute or two, and when that time is up, you will get more. You always will. And in time you will notice that the kindness you were hoping to receive from another will come, either from them, another source or from deep within you.

Be mindful of and open to all the generosity that came your way today; The smile of the store clerk, the lightening of your heart hearing a baby laugh, the wet nose of your dog, or the purring of your cat.

Make every effort to receive those acts of generosity with grace even if you've had a horrible day and cannot fully be in touch with the joy being offered. And have confidence that you will do better tomorrow.

And if for some understandable reason you aren't feeling particularly graceful or kind, fake it anyway. You'll do better tomorrow. Faking kindness is always better than indulging in grumpiness, because it will bring you closer to being genuinely generous tomorrow.

Do your best to approach everything in your life with grace and kindness, including every doorknob, sock, or chicken wing. There is no magic wand. Just us. And we are more than enough.

Jerzy M. Kokurewicz

GROW WISE

W isdom is not acquired. It blossoms, unbidden and unhurried. The practices of Honesty, Humility, Courage, Respect and Generosity are the fertile ground where Wisdom grows its deep roots.

You know your values. You know your place in the universe. You have faced your shadows. You have empathized with the shadows of others without judgment. And you are kind, even when you've had to fudge it from time to time.

That's all that wisdom really is. An honest and kind answer to a sincere question with no strings attached. "I don't know" is often the wisest response to any inquiry. Letting go of beliefs, and only speaking about what we know and have experienced is the only way to nurture wisdom.

Practice these phrases:

"I don't know." "What do you think?" "Uh-huh."

Seriously! Repeat them a hundred times a day if you have to, so that you become completely comfortable with the depth of wisdom within each of those phrases. Say those phrases like you mean them and someday it will be okay to realize that it *is perfectly fine to not know. In the end none of us has any idea what is truly going on. It's just all too complex.*

Stop. Take a breath. Listen to the whispers of Life. Repeat.

Don't worry. When the need arises (and it will), out of your mouth will flow the exact words that need to be heard in that moment by the anxious ears of the one in need. You will see that this unbidden wisdom will be there every single time, if you just stand out of its way.

And if you are lucky, you will have no memory of what came out of your mouth and you will be able to exit gracefully with your humility intact.

Do you think that the nightingale remembers its song? Not at all! It just fills its little lungs and sings another one.

Do not fear sounding stupid, because to your ears just about everything you have to say will sound inane and ridiculous, particularly if your ego is sufficiently out of the way and not prompting you to sound smart.

However, the miracle is that when you are speaking full-heartedly and unfiltered, someone somewhere is going to hear the wisdom they need to make more sense of their life.

Just sing your song and let it go.

LOVE UNCONDITIONALLY

Warning! Here's a concept that might set your teeth on edge. But please hang in there to the end.

There are no higher or lower forms of Love. When you boil it down to the bones there is no such thing as 'Pure Love', 'Motherly Love', 'Sexual Love', 'Platonic Love', or any other kind of 'Blah-blah Love'. There is just Love. That's it. End of story.

Remember this: Love isn't Love unless it's unconditional. Any action that has any hope for a particular result or any agenda stains its essence. Therefore, cannot be Love.

One expression of that principle is what I heard the Mi'kmaq Grandmothers of Turtle Island say. "There is no such thing as a bad person. There is only someone that needs healing, or someone that needs teaching."

We all have the capacity to love unconditionally once the shadows of our pain begin to loosen their grip on us.

The tricky thing is that Unconditional Love must begin with us. We have to learn to love ourselves when we fall short of our values. We have to learn to love ourselves even when we need to puff ourselves up to cover up our pain. We have to *learn to love ourselves when we are paralyzed with fear. We have to learn to love ourselves when we forget to be kind. We have to learn to love ourselves when we recklessly consume the sacrifices made on our behalf without a thought. We have to learn to love ourselves when we do something stupid. And we have to learn to love ourselves when we feel that we have sunk so low in our own esteem that we couldn't even tickle a worm's belly.*

The miracle is that even as we struggle with all our shortcomings and failures, and are blinded by the mists of our own despair, we are always loved by that Something or Other that has lovingly ordered this Universe specifically for our survival. The dependable existence of the gifts of air, earth, fire, and water are ample evidence of that Love.

My Elder, William, told me many, many times "You need to love everybody, even if you don't like them."

What makes his admonition so remarkable is his direct experience of extreme oppression and degradation. He confided in me his deep hatred of white people and yet, universally, all that came in contact with him felt his love and generosity even in the face of the disapproval of many of his native contemporaries.

That is unconditional love. He bestowed the same respect

and kindness on saints and stinkers alike. He did not allow his judgments to interfere. So his love flowed. He knew there was no other way. Many were blessed and comforted by his presence, and perhaps the seeds of reconciliation and love were planted in their hearts.

Unconditional love is in the air we breathe, the earth we walk on, the waters that cleanse us, and the warm glow of the fire that warms us and gives us light. When I follow the path that my values have laid out for me, I realize that I have no right to deny to another what has been so generously given to me.

I am no saint and I do get royally pissed off from time to time. The way I trick myself to love someone who has made me angry is this. I acknowledge in some 3-D, concrete way (such as some kind of ceremony, ritual or process including writing) how that person is my teacher and not my perpetrator. Thus, I am free to leave my victim conscience behind and reclaim my power. And if it's me that's tweaking me, I simply tell myself "Oh well. This is who I am today. If I was smart enough to do things any differently, I would have done it by now."

Admittedly, there are times when feeling like a victim seems to suit me. Luckily my unconditional love of self allows for that unfortunate state. That allowance helps me discover that the consequences of being a victim are not fun: with shaming and angry voices in my head, sourness in my stomach, and darkness that is felt by those close to me. My hope is that if I experience those uncomfortable consequences enough times I'll finally be willing to try something else.

Maybe I will and maybe I won't try the 'new thing' next time, but the doors will be open for me to make my choice and experience the consequences of my choice. Thus, by virtue of choice and responsibility, I retain my power and feel a hell of a lot better about myself regardless of any discomforting consequences.

A big part of moving into a state of unconditional love is leaving the victim behind. Victims do not have the ability to look at their supposed perpetrator and acknowledge that they are their teacher. However, faking it is a powerful tool. Use it.

So be Honest when the victim shadows you. Be Humble in accepting that is who you are today. Have the Courage to be willing to be free of resentment. Respect that everyone is at least as screwed up as you are if not more. Fake Generosity if you have to, look for the Wisdom laying at your feet like gold dust (it will be there), and finally enjoy the hell out of the Love that will inevitably blossom in your heart.

Love loves Love. And any tiny step you are able to take for Love's sake will help you make the most of the Earth-walk you have undertaken.

ODE'IMIN TEACHING

Strawberry Medicine

T his is a story that is told in the Lodge when we share a bowl of strawberries in-between rounds.

There were two brothers who were as close as two boys could be. They played together, learned to hunt and fish together, and spent all their time together. They were inseparable playing in the village and in the forest.

As they grew older, they grew stronger, sometimes not knowing their own strength. One day they were wrestling like they always did when one of the boys threw the other down so hard that he hit his head on a rock. In his pain, that boy was so angry that he picked up the rock and bashed it into the other one's head. That in turn made the first boy angry and they fought like they wanted to kill each other. Their Grandfather ran out to them and separated them before any more harm would come.

These boys were so angry at each other that they swore that they never wanted to lay eyes on the other again, and they both ran from the village crying, one this way and the other in the opposite direction.

The first boy that left the village walked for hours and hours, tears of anger and pain running down his face. "How could he have hurt me like that?" he said over and over again. After a while, the tears stopped, and he realized that he had wandered far in his anger and he didn't know where he was. And he started to wonder where his brother was, and if he was doing okay.

"Why did I get so angry? Where is my brother? I miss him and I wish he was here with me."

And the tears started again, but this time they were tears of regret and sorrow.

And so he walked on, head bowed low and crying.

Through his tears he saw something red in the grass that he had never seen before. He picked it up and saw that it was heart-shaped berry. Suddenly he realized that he had been gone so long that he was getting hungry, so he put the berry in his mouth and ate it.

It was sweet and delicious! And then he found another in the grass a few steps ahead of him. He picked and ate that one, too. As he walked forward, he found another and another one. He so enjoyed the sweetness of the berries that soon his tears dried up.

As he was going along he suddenly heard a shout, and looking up, he saw his brother coming towards him, eating berries just like he was.

With big shouts of joy, they ran to each other and embraced, vowing to never again abandon each other in rage and pain.

That is why, in the language of the Anishinabek people a strawberry is called the heart-berry. It carries the Medicine of Reconciliation and reminds us that even at the lowest times of our lives, when we are crying with our heads hanging low, we can always find the sweetness of life through our tears. It will always be there no matter what.

Unconditional Love is not only what we try to practice, but it is also what we must always try to receive.

Jerzy M. Kokurewicz

EPILOGUE

The heavy mists of the night were beginning to hide the dense jungle of Tikal until only the tops of the temples were visible above the clouds.

From where I stood at the pinnacle of Temple IV all the stone summits were gray and dark. Except one. It glowed with a phosphorescent green above the tree tops.

I heard howler monkeys howl and jaguars growl as I prepared to spend a sleepless night in the cold stony darkness of my refuge.

At least this time I did not have a uniformed guard pointing a gun at my face.

From the next book in the series:

Sacred EarthWalk: Stories on the Journey

ABOUT THE AUTHOR.

Jerzy Kokurewicz is the Author of the **"Sacred EarthWalk"** book series that come from the life he has lived and the stories of his journey from then until now.

You can learn more about the author in his forthcoming book, **"Sacred EarthWalk: Stories along the Journey"**, and at his website here

https://www.jerzymkokurewicz.com

REFERENCE

---

1. **The Mishomis Book - The Voice of the Ojibway** *is published by:*
Indian Country Communications, Inc.
8558N County Road K
Hayward, Wisconsin 54843
Ph. 715-634-5226
www.IndianCountryNews.com
and is available on Amazon.

2. *http://www.SevenGrandfatherTeachings.com*

Jerzy M. Kokurewicz

www.ingramcontent.com/pod-product-compliance
Lightning Source LLC
Chambersburg PA
CBHW060909280326
41934CB00007B/1253